Enoch Speaks from Heaven:

A Divine Revelation

Nicola Whitehall

Matthew Robert Payne

0 1 2 3 4 5 6 7 8 9 1 0

Dedications

MATTHEW

I dedicate this book to Darla.

Darla has loved me and my books from a distance. I have not had many lengthy conversations with her, but I know she is full of love for me and my work. She also helps do the design work on each of my books now.

NICOLA

I dedicate this book to Ferrell.

She has continually encouraged me and provided reality checks when I put too much of my ego into my writing. Thanks for steering me straight. Your appreciation and feedback on what I have shared with you has kept me writing. May God bless you in every way. You are a remarkable and highly gifted woman.

Table of Contents

Matthew's Questions

QUESTION 1:

How do you feel about being here today?

Enoch: I'm very happy to be with you again. I have visited you a number of times since you've been walking with the Lord. You and I have spent some time together. I've visited with Elijah, and both of us have walked and talked with you. I came down and did an interview with you for the book, *Great Cloud of Witnesses Speak*, and you produced that interview and book with Elijah and me, along with another book about the two witnesses. We have spent some time together, and we've come to know each other.

It's a real joy to be here. Part of the reason for this question at the beginning of all your interviews is to first help you relax and be at peace and comfortable so that you can interview us saints. It's hard to transition from just being a normal saint who is living day-to-day to someone who's bringing the voice and the recordings of other saints from heaven. In the same way, it takes some concentration and anointing to bring the voice of Jesus to someone else through the gift of prophecy. It takes anointing and understanding to bring the voice of a saint to other people.

I understand the transition and concentration that you need. You have to be at peace and relaxed. I'm happy to be here with you and to encourage you that everything will be fine. I have waited a number of years for this opportunity to come down and speak to the people of earth. You have developed Nicola to a point where she is comfortable interviewing saints with you, and this will be your second book with her. It's exciting for her to do an interview with me.

I'm so happy that you've reached out to her and included her voice, a woman's perspective, in the interview process. Heaven and the Holy Spirit gave you the idea to include her so that you could do books together. She's very talented at hearing from God and is learning to hear from saints. It's a real joy to have her as part of the team that's producing these books.

I'm excited to be here and to speak through you. I'm happy that you're becoming relaxed and more at ease as my voice flows through you. I enjoy watching you stretch your faith and place your hands in the hands of the Holy Spirit. You now trust the Holy Spirit to an extent that you step out and do these interviews as led by him and by the Father.

It's a real honor to be on earth, standing in your kitchen behind you during this interview. I enjoy your house. It's cleaner now than it used to be, and it's a nice environment.

Many angels are in your house, and it feels heavenly. I came through the portal in your kitchen today with easy access. I feel at ease with you, and I'm quite ready to speak. Let's continue with the rest of the interview.

QUESTION 2:

How did you enjoy your time on earth?

Enoch: Before the term mystic became popular, before people started using the word, I was a mystic. I was responsible for writing the book of Enoch, which you've read, Matthew. It's confusing to you.

You really didn't enjoy reading it and didn't want to read it for the second time to prepare for this interview. But I saw and experienced some remarkable and amazing things when I was on earth.

I was truly a friend of God's. I guess I want to highlight that you can pursue God and pursue an intimate relationship with him, and God will open up the heavens to you. The closer you are to your Creator, the more you can experience his creation.

Just imagine that you were trained in physics and that you came across a physicist. You befriended this famous physicist and went out for coffee with him and became his closest friend. If this physicist really loved you and opened up his heart to you, he would tell you about his explorations and about science in a way that not many real physicists would get to see. Of course, he'd have his journals for mankind, which is the Bible to the average Christian. But this physicist would take you inside and personally share his mind and discoveries with you. You'd know this physicist in a way that no other person has known him. The same is true with God.

You can have a superficial relationship with God, a relationship that consists of going to church on Sunday, reading your Bible occasionally, and praying one-way prayers. When I say one-way prayers, I am referring to the fact that most Christians pray a prayer and just speak to God without allowing him to speak back to them. A majority of Christians prays these one-way prayers. They go to church on Sunday. They read the Bible from time to time, which is the extent of their relationship with God.

I had a much deeper relationship with God and spoke with him every day. We were sharing intimate visitations and encounters. I actually spent so much time in heaven while I walked the earth that God just got sick of me going back to earth and invited me to heaven permanently. I became so close to God that God didn't want to be separated from me anymore. I walked into heaven, and I've been in his company ever since.

3

My life on earth was enjoyable, but the focal point of my life was God and my relationship with him. I want to stress to you, reader, that you can grow really close to God. There's no limit to how close you can become to him. You can deepen your relationship with him. The deeper that you grow, the more of his kingdom that he'll show you.

Matthew has grown to the point where he encounters angels and saints from heaven. He has regular visits to heaven. He's grown to a place where God will come to earth and fellowship and commune with him. He still has so much room for growth. My relationship with God on earth was paramount, which allowed me to experience joy and ecstasy.

The modern grace movement focuses on joy and ecstasy, which is wonderful. People enter ecstatic encounters and sometimes go into trances and get caught up and have visions. I was getting caught up so often that many people just saw me disappear. I wanted nothing but God. I had no carnal desire for the things of earth. One touch from God, and I was sold.

My life was radically different from the lives of many of the readers of this book. Many of you are focused on work, family, possessions, status, and politics. So many people are tightly caught up with the world. I was caught up with God.

A common saying follows: "Don't be so heavenly minded that you're no earthly good." I disagree with this cliché. You need to be so heavenly minded that it affects everything that you do on earth. It's not true that you are no earthly good when you're heavenly minded. The reverse is true: you become very useful to the people on the earth when you have access to the mind of God, access to heaven and heaven's beings.

I enjoyed my time on earth but can't compare it to the average Christian's life on earth. I lived a totally different life from the majority of Christians. This life is possible. It's mystical, a life of visions, encounters, trances, and supernatural experiences. You can enter into this life that I lived, and you can press in and go after God with all of your heart, mind, and soul.

Mary Magdalene, the Apostle Paul, and some of the saints mentioned through history have touched on this life. But I breathe a rarified air, which is a totally different encounter than the average Christian has with God. I encourage you to pursue God with everything that you have within you.

QUESTION 3:

What is your experience of heaven?

Enoch: Let me just start by saying that heaven is my home. Every person who is reading this book comes from a family. Some of you had a loving father; some of you did not have such a loving father, but everyone started in a family.

Imagine if you had the most loving and supportive, generous, kind father, and you lived a life where everything was given to you, every desire met, and you were encouraged, trained up, and financed until you became a responsible adult. You would always treasure your relationship with your father. You'd always treasure going home to your father's house. Well, that's the state, the life, I have in heaven in my Father's house.

I grew up with a God that loved, affirmed, reassured, encouraged, supported, and backed me. He spiritually financed me and gave me self-esteem. My esteem was placed firmly on who I was to God. I live in heaven with my Father, my Papa. He makes heaven so beautiful. I'm so loved, but the concept of feeling so at home with my Heavenly Father might be foreign to people who didn't have a good experience with their own father.

No matter where you come from, no matter your experience, you can go through inner healing so that you come to a place where you're open to accept the love of the Father, the love of

Father God. I'm at ease in heaven and totally accepted and free to do as my heart desires. I'm affirmed, encouraged, supported, backed, led, and cherished by God.

Are those factors true in your life? Is that true of your experience with God? Does he love you in a whole wonderful dimension? Do you feel totally supported by him?

I live a life in heaven where I experience the joy of the Lord every day. I live in ecstasy, and I enjoy doing different things that keep me totally engrossed in what I'm meant to do.

We're going to cover what I do in heaven in question five. I'm just sharing a little bit about my experience with heaven here. I will be sharing more later.

The Father loves me with tremendous love, and so does Jesus. When you're totally loved, when you're totally accepted, when your whole being is accepted by God and by Jesus, you can do marvelous things. When you are given tasks and assignments by God and he's confident that you can achieve them, you can do nothing but be successful. After all, he designed the actual task for you to do.

It's so different from your world. Your world is hard and complicated, and people sometimes struggle to find out the will of God and find direction in life. It's sometimes quite difficult for you to feel that God supports you and gives you a task that is straight from the throne room and straight from his mouth.

Many people on earth wander from place to place and assignment to assignment, unsure that they're directed by God. So many people on earth don't hear from God. So many Christians on earth can't speak and can't hear God's will. In contrast, heaven is so different. Being directed by the Holy Spirit on earth is a rarity for many Christians, but in heaven, part of the culture is to be directed by the Holy Spirit. It's amazing to be in a place where you're totally supported, entirely directed by

God, and able to exercise your unique gifts and talents to do what benefits all of heaven, God, and Jesus.

I receive a lot of support and encouragement from my Father in heaven. I shine with an amazing glory, which is out of this world. Some people in heaven just see me as a light being. I shine so brightly.

My experience of heaven is being in a place where everything you do, everything you touch, turns to gold, like the Midas touch. It's pretty amazing to live your life on earth in such a place where everything you touch and do turns to gold. Psalm 1:3 says, "He shall be like a tree planted by the rivers of water, that brings forth its fruit in its season, whose leaf also shall not wither; and whatever he does shall prosper." That's a picture of the life that you can live on earth if you take the time and make the effort to get to know God, learn to hear his voice, and learn how to be directed by the Holy Spirit in everything you do and say.

QUESTION 4:

What do you like about heaven?

Enoch: One of the things I like most about heaven is that anything is possible there. If you can dream it or think it, if your intellect or your mind thinks of something in heaven, it can be done. Even the impossible can be done in heaven. An exciting aspect of heaven is that your mind can come up with creative ideas, and then you can put them into practice and implement them and create and do spectacular things in heaven.

On earth, you seem to have limitations. You need money, resources, people, and structures. In heaven, there are no limitations, no monetary restraints, or even restraints from people. There are no real restraints in heaven. We don't deal with selfishness or greed. So much of earth revolves around the greed and the selfishness of the community. So many limitations are placed on what can be done on earth because of men's selfishness and greed. This doesn't exist in heaven.

If someone is successful in heaven, that doesn't mean someone else is a failure. One person's success in heaven doesn't come at someone else's expense. Someone succeeding in heaven doesn't come through climbing over another person. That's not how you get to the top in heaven. It's a different culture there. People are honored, trusted, and given responsibility in heaven.

It's just a different dimension to live in. It's similar to earth, because you have desires, and you can exercise your gifts and use your talents to glorify mankind and God in heaven. I like the fact that things aren't impossible in heaven.

I like the idea that there are no limitations in heaven. People in heaven are shown the truth. Error doesn't exist at all in heaven. Heaven has no false teachings.

Just consider how much false teaching you have come out of in your life. How much error have you believed in the past, and how did that error limit you? In heaven, that doesn't exist. There are no limitations. People understand the truth in heaven and go from one truth to the next, one truth to a greater manifestation of that truth, into a greater glory of that truth. They grow exponentially in heaven. (See 2 Corinthians 3:18.)

Heaven is a learning environment, a remarkable place where you can dream of how you want to live and then live your dreams. You want to end up there and live your life for Jesus and be committed to him for the rest of your days. Make sure that you do what is necessary to come to heaven because you will really enjoy it there. There are no limits.

You can drive a vehicle at light speed through heaven without crashing into anything. You can imagine that you want to be somewhere else in heaven, as far as America is from Africa, and you could appear on a different continent within a second. Within a blink of an eye, you could go from

America to Africa, which you can do on earth too. People can translocate like that, but it's a lot rarer on earth than it is in heaven.

Michael Van Vlymen. in his book, *Supernatural Transportation: Moving Through Space, Time and Dimension for the Kingdom of Heaven*, speaks about translating from place to place and how he has done that. In heaven, you can do that all the time. You can travel on a bus, a train, a car, or in a spaceship in heaven, or you can just instantly appear where you want to be. If you enjoy travel, you can travel by any means that you desire, or if you just want to appear there instantly, you can do that instead.

There's so much to learn about heaven. Kat Kerr in her books, *Revealing Heaven: An Eyewitness Account* and *Revealing Heaven 2*, shares quite a bit about heaven and what it's like, but what I like most about heaven is the lack of limits. That truly has to be understood to be appreciated.

People, such as Joyce Meyer, Andrew Wommack, and Benny Hinn, enjoy a world where they have had open doors and success, and yet they still face limitations. They still suffer with lack. They still have needs and demands on their ministry. Even though they're in the will of God, even though God supplies all their needs, they still have desires that require more money.

If they were given double the money that they currently have, they could easily spend it because they have so many things they are planning to do. In heaven, there are no limitations, and you really need to ponder that because it makes heaven unique.

QUESTION 5:

What do you do in heaven?

Enoch: I am doing various things in heaven. I enjoy being a tour guide in heaven, both in heaven itself and in galaxies around the universe. Many people realize that I've traveled to galaxies and to different destinations if they've read the book of Enoch.

I take some of the hungry people that come to heaven on tours. I even take people that are on earth on tours of the galaxies. People who are advanced can contact me, see me, and travel with me. I take them on tours.

I like being a tour guide. I have a lot of information about other galaxies, other planets, and other places in the universe. I have a lot of information about things and places in heaven and places of special importance and secrets in heaven. These are complex places, places of uniqueness with special reasons as to why they exist.

One of the jobs that I love to do is taking people on tours. I love dealing with hungry people; they're my favorite people. You don't necessarily have to be advanced in the kingdom and translating everywhere and healing the sick to be hungry. Even a new baby Christian can be hungry. I enjoy and love hunger in a person.

If you have hungered after the things of God, I would really like to meet you, and I'd like to take you on a tour and show you things in your mind. I can show you different destinations, and you can travel in the spirit with me. Kat Kerr is seeing a lot of places and has been taken to special places. If she were allowed to do so, she could take people on tours to those places and show people the purposes and designs of different places. She hasn't been commissioned to do that right now. But I can and I do. That's one of the things I do in heaven.

Certain councils sit in heaven, a select group of prophets, apostles, and former saints. People who are living on earth and who are in authority there sit on councils and decide the future of heaven and earth. These particular councils exist for different reasons. I've been part of these councils, just like a board of directors. I oversee decisions made in heaven and on earth. I sit on some of these councils and lend my expertise and my weight into them. You might have heard of certain saints who visited heaven, speaking about councils on earth. I've encountered certain councils in heaven, and prophet Sadhu Sundar Selvaraj from earth has sat on some of these councils and been part of them.

A large part of my responsibilities is to act as an ascended master, to use a new age term. I'm used by God to do spectacular things and weigh in with my thoughts on these special heavenly councils that have been set up.

I like to paint in heaven, which would shock a few people. I painted in heaven, and I do different forms of painting. In heaven, there are different styles of painting, including landscapes. When you paint a landscape in heaven, an angel will take you to a place in heaven that's just been created to look exactly like what you just painted.

In the paintings that I've done, I've created places in different galaxies, and in heaven, I'm a creator; all the artists there are. That's one of the joys of heaven for me.

These are some of the things I am doing in heaven. I certainly enjoy myself. I really enjoy my relationship with Jesus and the Father there. I'll be speaking more about that in questions six and seven.

Painting really relaxes me. It's not that you need to be relaxed in heaven, because heaven is so peaceful, but you can escape and create there. I've become a great painter in heaven with some excellent paintings. I have a studio where people can come and select my art work and hang it in their houses. Perhaps if you come to heaven, you can one day own one of my paintings.

11

If you're hungry enough and if you pursue God enough, perhaps you can sit on one of the councils with me. I might also be able to show you a part of heaven as a tour guide. I'm also involved in teaching, learning, and participating in mystical activities in heaven. I've just covered a few of the basics here, but my life in heaven is a whole lot more complex.

QUESTION 6:

What is your relationship with Jesus like in heaven?

Enoch: Mary Magdalene explained this quite well in the book, *Mary Magdalene Speaks from Heaven: Book 2*. The whole of heaven swings on the axis of Jesus Christ, revolving on him. Jesus is the center of heaven. You won't enjoy heaven if you don't have a strong relationship with Jesus. I have an amazing, intimate relationship with him. It's so good to have loved God and then met his Son.

When I was on earth, I only knew God. But when Jesus died on the cross, he came to heaven, and I came to know him. He always existed in heaven pre-incarnate, but I only seem to have known God when I lived on earth. That might be hard for people to understand. It's even hard for Matthew to comprehend.

Have you ever met a man with tremendous leadership skills, who is amazing in business, who's very successful at everything he does, who is warm and loving with a wonderful wife, who really carries himself well? Then one day, after years of knowing this man, you finally meet his son who was overseas. The son is a representation of the father. There are so many similarities between the son and the father. Then you find yourself loving the son just as much as you love the father. That's how it was for me when I met Jesus. I knew his Father so well that meeting Jesus was amazing, and I have a tremendous respect and honor for Jesus.

Jesus has become a very close and intimate friend to me. We walk through heaven together. Indeed, everyone who's in heaven walks through heaven with Jesus from time to time. Matthew has mentioned this in other interviews that he's done with saints. If you're a believer and you make it to heaven, you will have one-on-one time with Jesus and be able to spend time with him.

Part of being in heaven is having a relationship with Jesus. I've walked hand in hand with Jesus in heaven. He has been part of some of the councils in heaven, and we've developed a larger, professional board room, a relationship with each other in those positions. Jesus is on some of the councils but only weighs in as one person. His opinion doesn't carry any extra weight there.

He is just a part of the councils and doesn't run them. That's the beauty of heaven. Heaven delegates power and official authority to individuals. Those individuals responsibly carry and delegate that authority as it's been given to them.

Jesus and I are very close friends. He kisses and hugs me. He walks hand in hand with me. He held my attention and held my face in his arms, in his hands. He speaks wonderful things to me. Princess Diana spoke eloquently in Matthew's book, *Princess Diana Speaks from Heaven*. She talked about her relationship with Jesus. I find myself comparing my response here with her response, and I encourage you to read what she said. I really enjoy Jesus.

He's everything to me. My life wouldn't be complete without Jesus in it. He carries tremendous burdens for the world. He suffers so much pain, and it's comforting to speak with him face-to-face and help him address his pain and deal with some of the issues that are causing him pain in some of the councils that we sit on. You can have such a special relationship with Jesus when he opens up and shares his pain with you. I understand that side of him. I have been involved with him and spoken to him about it, which gives me a special insight into him that few people see or even recognize or acknowledge.

Many people on earth have no idea that Jesus suffers and has tremendous pain watching and having to put up with what's happening on earth: from child trafficking, slavery, and the injustices that are happening, to the poor, the pain, the suffering, the sickness, and everything caused by the curse and by the selfishness of men and Satan. Jesus really suffers. So it's good to be able to speak to him, down by the Crystal Sea, walking hand in hand and comforting him as he cries. I consider being a close and personal friend to Jesus an important part of my ministry in heaven.

QUESTION 7:

What is your relationship with the Father in heaven?

Enoch: I love God. I love Papa God. He is my source. The passion that's in my heart beats for God. I love him so completely, and like his Son, Jesus, he suffers and experiences pain. Can you just imagine if you were a father with six girls who were kidnapped and forced into prostitution? What if you knew they were prostitutes and that ten men were sleeping with each of them every day, but you could do nothing about it? How would that make you feel as a father? Well, that's how God feels about trafficked people on earth. That's how he feels about people in sickness and with illnesses, and that's how he feels about poverty and injustice.

God is a God who cares, and he has a very passionate and loving heart. God so loved the world that he gave his only Son, that whoever believes in Jesus would not die but have eternal life. (See John 3:16.) Jesus came to earth and was manifested to take away the sins of the world. The Father expressed his love by giving his Son to the earth. His Son lived a model and an exemplary life and then suffered on the cross for the salvation of men. Only the love of the Father would send his Son to be crucified.

I know this Father, this loving Father, and I know his intimate secrets. I know things that I can't tell you here because people wouldn't believe them. I know information about the world and the future that I can't share here. People wouldn't believe it. People would be so surprised at what I said. This information would shock too many people. People would dismiss what I have to say.

These are things that the Father tells me and shows me. I know wonderful things. I know that the Father has a really big smile on his face when he speaks of Donald Trump. When Donald Trump's name is mentioned, the Father smiles with joy. He knows that Donald is rough around the edges. He knows that Donald says some pretty outrageous things, but he loves Donald's heart.

I relate to my Father in heaven as a son would relate to a loving father. I'm accepted as a son in heaven, with all the birthrights of a son. The Father is like a king, and I'm like a prince. I have the authority of a prince in heaven. I work with the authority of the Father in heaven and decree things that come to pass on earth. I make decisions that happen on earth. I'm involved in the councils of heaven and directed by the Holy Spirit. I affect change on earth with some of what I do. We also need prophets from earth as part of the councils in heaven to decree things on earth. We have someone from earth who sits in the councils who then brings these decrees back to earth.

It might be hard for you to understand the love I have for God in heaven. Many of you might not have walked in the level of love that I have for the Father. I cherish him. He cherishes me. I respect him. He respects me. I honor him. He honors me. I lift him up. He lifts me up. It's like looking into a mirror. I look into the Father's eyes, and I see myself. He looks into my eyes, and he sees me reflected in him. I've become one with the Father. We walk in oneness together. (See John 17.)

It's hard to contemplate, but I've become one of the most perfect saints in heaven. I live in another realm. I'm speaking today in simple language, simple language that Matthew and his readers can understand. But I live at another level, another sphere of influence, at another level of understanding, which is far beyond that of most people on earth.

You realize that I wrote the book of Enoch thousands of years ago. That's beyond the understanding of most people, and I've spent thousands of years in heaven, so my intellect and my knowledge of the things of God far surpasses that of most Christians on earth. Yet my relationship with the Father has been growing throughout all those years. I've become a mighty prince and a mighty authority in heaven. I exercise and enjoy that authority. I enjoy my intimate relationship with the Father, and I enjoy speaking to you and sharing some of this information.

QUESTION 8:

Who do you enjoy most, the Father or Jesus, and why?

Enoch: Let's compare two men. The first is a businessman, your contemporary and the successful owner of a multinational company. You worked for another company, and you came to know him, fellowshipping at his house, going out for coffee with him, eating meals together, and sitting on his board. You really grew to love him. Then one day, you meet his son, who is now the CEO of the company, and you develop a relationship with the son. Who would you love more, the father or the son?

The son would be loved and become special to you, but your original love is for the father. All the love you have for the son would be because you love his father. It would be quite unusual for you to surpass the love you have for the father. The father could pass away, and then you might develop the same sort of love for the son, but you probably would still favor the father.

I share this analogy to say that I chiefly love God. It's hard to compare the Father and the Son, but Matthew asked this question to make a point. You could probably tell in my answers to questions six and seven about Jesus and the Father that I adored the Father more. It's only a small difference. I admire and love Jesus with an intimate relationship, with an intimate love. Yet I grew up loving his Father and loving that relationship more.

Matthew's different. He loves Jesus more than the Father and is more intimate with Jesus than he is with the Father. It's not wrong for one love to be a little stronger than the other. It's just the way that things are, but the difference is really slight and minute. I could have said that I love them equally, which could be true. If that is true, you might not be lying, but the truth is the love that I have for Jesus comes from the love that I have for his Father. Jesus will always be the Son to me, revealed as a son. The current CEO, the leader and the head of the company, is always the son to me.

Matthew becomes a bit nervous about these answers, thinking, *how will people take this? Will they relate to it, or will they reject it, saying that you can't have a stronger love for one more than the other? How could someone love the Father more than Jesus?* Nearly every Christian varies in their love for the Father and Jesus with their love for one stronger than their love for the other. It's also true for me in heaven.

I enjoy, revere, honor, and love Jesus. My love for Jesus far surpasses the love that anyone on earth has for him. I guess that people on earth would have to reach another dimension to get to my level. That sounds like pride speaking, but it's just the truth. If you've spent thousands of years in the company of Jesus and you grow to the ascended state that I am, you will love Jesus a whole lot more than someone who's only had eighty years of knowing him compared to thousands of years. It might sound like pride, but I'm just speaking the truth here. I hope you enjoyed my answer.

QUESTION 9:

Is there any reason to fear the coming tribulation?

Enoch: Jesus shared in Matthew 7 that a wise man built his house upon the rock. Jesus then goes on to say that a person is a wise man when he hears what Jesus taught and builds his life upon those teachings. Jesus says that person is wise because his life is based on Jesus's teachings. When the storm comes, the house won't be demolished because it's built on the rock.

Jesus then says that a foolish man built his house upon the sand. He identifies a foolish person as someone who hears the teachings of Jesus but ignores them and doesn't build his life upon those teachings. Scripture states that the rains and the storm come, and the house falls and is washed away, and great is its fall. That's a scripture, that's the warning to people who are going to face the coming tribulation.

Now I know that many great teachers teach that there won't be a tribulation, a rapture, or an antichrist. I'm aware of who is teaching these things, but we're not talking about them.

A tribulation will come, and the people who are walking in the Spirit and obeying Jesus will be directed and protected by them. But if you aren't living your life according to the teachings of Jesus, you're not in a safe position. When the storm comes and the rain descends, your house will fall. You have reason to fear if you're not obeying Jesus. Jesus gave fifty commands in the Bible, and you can find them by looking them up on Google. You can learn more about what Jesus taught in Matthew's book, *The Parables of Jesus Made Simple: Updated and Expanded Edition*. The more that you learn about Jesus and his teachings and the more that you start to practice and live your life according to his teachings, the less you'll have to fear from the coming tribulation.

Darkness is coming to the world. People are moving toward a state of lawlessness and starting to do all kinds of weird things. You can expect unusual things to begin to happen. The fundamental teachings of the Bible are being ignored and trampled on, and it's just going to grow worse and worse. A time will come when an anti-Christ will be elected, and he will wipe out the money supply. He will pursue Christians and try to kill them. You will need to hear from the Holy Spirit. You will need to be directed by Jesus himself so that you can get to a safe place, a place of refuge.

Christians will be able to go to places of refuge, safe places on the earth where they can reside and live comfortably. God will provide for them just like he provided for and fed the children of Israel in the wilderness. God can easily do that again, and he can multiply food and do all kinds of miracles to help people. It really comes down to you.

Are you willing to learn how to hear God's voice? Are you willing to put in the time to learn how to hear from God right now? Matthew wrote a book on how to hear God's voice called, *How to Hear God's Voice: Keys to Two-Way Conversational Prayer,* and which you can order to learn more. Will you learn how to hear God's voice and how to listen to God? Will you learn to journal and hear from God each day? Will you take the time to learn how to walk in the Spirit and follow his directions each day?

If you take those steps, then you'll be safe with nothing to fear. There'll be nothing that you can't survive. If you choose not to learn how to hear God's voice, if you willingly disobey what Jesus taught, if you ignore my warning in this book, and if you just blindly go on with your Christian life without concern for your future, you might be caught and lose your life because of what's coming.

I guess what I'm saying is that there's a way to be close to God. There's a way to be obedient to Jesus by walking in his will and being directed by him each day. There's also a way to disobey

God and Jesus and not hear from Jesus or the Holy Spirit or be directed by them. This puts your life in jeopardy.

QUESTION 10:

What is your future role on earth?

Enoch: Revelation 11:1–14 shares a prophecy of John about my future on earth. I'll just put this scripture here, and we'll talk about it.

"Then I was given a reed like a measuring rod. And the angel stood, saying, 'Rise and measure the temple of God, the altar, and those who worship there. But leave out the court which is outside the temple, and do not measure it, for it has been given to the Gentiles. And they will tread the holy city underfoot for forty-two months. And I will give power to my two witnesses, and they will prophesy one thousand two hundred and sixty days, clothed in sackcloth.'

"These are the two olive trees and the two lampstands standing before the God of the earth. And if anyone wants to harm them, fire proceeds from their mouth and devours their enemies. And if anyone wants to harm them, he must be killed in this manner. These have power to shut heaven, so that no rain falls in the days of their prophecy; and they have power over waters to turn them to blood, and to strike the earth with all plagues, as often as they desire.

"When they finish their testimony, the beast that ascends out of the bottomless pit will make war against them, overcome them, and kill them. And their dead bodies will lie in the street of the great city which spiritually is called Sodom and Egypt, where also our Lord was crucified. Then those from the peoples, tribes, tongues, and nations will see their dead bodies three-and-a-half days, and not allow their dead bodies to be put into graves. And those who dwell on the earth will rejoice over them, make merry, and send gifts to one another, because these two prophets tormented those who dwell on the earth.

"Now after the three-and-a-half days the breath of life from God entered them, and they stood on their feet, and great fear fell on those who saw them. And they heard a loud voice from heaven saying to them, 'Come up here.' And they ascended to heaven in a cloud, and their enemies saw them. In the same hour there was a great earthquake, and a tenth of the city fell. In the earthquake seven thousand people were killed, and the rest were afraid and gave glory to the God of heaven.

"The second woe is past. Behold, the third woe is coming quickly."

A time will come when I physically return to earth. I'm in a physical body while in heaven now. I'm not in a spiritual body, and I'll appear fully grown on earth in the future. Elijah and I will have physical bodies, and we'll start to minister, prophesy, and do healings and miracles and judge the world. We will hold different countries accountable and tell them to do certain things.

If they don't do what we ask, plagues and judgments will come against them. We'll quickly have the attention of the world and the media. Every day on television screens all around the world, they will play our prophecies and judgments at the same time. The worldwide church will see us through the work of the 144,000 mentioned in the Bible. This number represents many passionate Christians, more than 144,000. The actual number is larger. Those passionate Christians will bring the kingdom to earth and preach and win souls for the Lord. Compared with them, we will be preaching the message of Jesus and his righteousness and his kingdom. We will work with those people and will draw the world to make a decision for Christ.

At the same time, the anti-Christ will be operating and pursuing Christians and trying to put them to death. He will bring in the mark of the beast. The anti-Christ will promote Satan's agenda and the deep state's agenda, but we will be operating in God's agenda. The global population will be faced with making a decision.

Like you've seen in the United States, God can bring an elected leader into a country, such as Donald Trump. Half the country can be bitterly opposed to God's elected leader. Some Christians in the United States even fight against him. He's God's leader. If they listen to the prophets and to God and if they can hear from him, they'll know that Donald is the elected leader of the nation and God's appointed man. But many can't hear from God, and they refuse to listen to their prophets, so they are against him.

The same will be true for the two of us. No matter how many signs, wonders, judgments, and plagues we do, a certain element of people will refuse to believe that we are from God.

Just like people who are Democrats and Christians in the United States are opposed to Donald Trump, some Christians, leaders of organizations, and others will be opposed to everything we do. Revelation 11:7–8 says we will be killed and lie on the streets of Jerusalem for three days. The whole world will start another Christmas, giving each other gifts because the prophets who caused such torment in the world have now died.

They will all celebrate as if it's Christmas. We would've judged the world so harshly and brought so many countries under the submission of God through his judgments. Many of the people in the world will hate us. It's been our pleasure to live in heaven for thousands of years and to be built up and involved in the councils of heaven. We have the understanding of God and of Jesus. We are ready to come to earth now.

We've had all that built up so that when we come to earth, we'll execute judgment. We will know all the specific companies in the world that can be changed and given directions to change, those that are good and those that are evil.

We will know all the corrupt politicians. We will have all that information, and we'll be able to bring justice to the world. Just as the Democrats hate the Republicans and Donald Trump, people will hate us.

Many people will try and kill us, including snipers who shoot bullets. Bullets will veer off our heads and won't be able to kill us. Despite their attacks, we will survive until our mission is accomplished, and we are killed on the streets of Jerusalem.

We will travel the globe. Many prophets believe that we will just be in Jerusalem, but we will travel from country to country and address the leaders of countries and the media. We will stir up the world. Matthew has a book that speaks more about our role in the world, *Optimistic Visions of Revelation*. You can learn more about what we'll be doing and our role in the earth in that book.

It's been my pleasure and my honor to be here. I hope you've enjoyed the answers to my questions, and I look forward to seeing you in heaven one day.

Nicola's Questions

QUESTION 1:

How do you feel about being here today?

Enoch: I'm very excited about being here today, Nicola. I am looking forward to speaking to you. I have a real admiration for you and how you keep going and persevere through the hard times, despite the evil and the wickedness that comes against you in the spiritual realm. I see the enemy's attacks on your mind and that you persist against those attacks. The Lord will help you remove the weakness in your mind, and you won't be as susceptible to those attacks anymore.

Nicola: Thank you, Enoch. How are you feeling today?

Enoch: I'm feeling really confident and buoyant. I have lots of interesting things planned to say to you today. I've read your questions. I know exactly what I'm going to say, and I know what I want the reader to hear. I'm just looking forward to starting the questions.

Nicola: Thank you, Enoch.

QUESTION 2:

What would you say to people who have read the book of Enoch?

Enoch: I would say that it can be a complex book. It contains lots of revelation for the person who's looking, for the real seekers. You can learn a lot from that book. The book is not for everyone; as you know, it's not easily understood. You found it quite hard to understand, and so did Matthew. But it has gems of revelation in it for those who are really seekers, the intellectual, and those who are into what I was talking about.

If people want to search out more, they can discover a lot, and a gold mine lies within the pages. Nothing can stop people from finding the revelation hidden in those words. As those people open themselves up to God, God will reveal the information to them, just as if you read between the lines of what someone says.

God will show you what he's really saying through me in the book of Enoch, and you can read between the lines. God will give you the hidden revelation, the hidden manna. It's like the manna in the desert. When Moses was leading the people of Israel through the desert, the manna that fell fed the people. So my book, for the right researcher, the right person, the person with the right kind of mind, has many gems and much value to it. I'm not going to give you any more insight into it. The people who want to research and look into it and want to receive revelation about it will do so, and I will assure them that they will receive a lot of richness from reading the book.

Nicola: Enoch, do you want to say anything else to the readers about the book of Enoch?

Enoch: No, Nicola. I've said almost everything I want to say about the subject, and I'm anxious to move on to the rest of the questions.

QUESTION 3:

What do you have to say to people who aren't Christians about what God is like?

Enoch: God is a fabulous God. He is beyond the comprehension of most people. They don't know the level of greatness that abounds in him. They don't know what is available for them in God. They have experienced such a limited perception of a father on this earth, what he is and what he does. Even people who have had good fathers don't have any perception of God as the perfect Father until they come to heaven and really begin to know him and what he offers them. He's a Father, but he's like no human being, like no one else on earth. You can't find anyone greater than the Father. He's just so amazing and awesome. You can't find anyone more trustworthy, more loving, more loyal, or more faithful. He will deliver you from every situation, trial, and suffering. Whether he takes you to heaven or delivers you on this earth varies for each person.

God has so much love to give, so much to offer, so much talent in so many areas. People don't think much about the talents that Father God has. Just as he puts talents in people, he has talents in himself, and he wants people to discover his talents too. He wants people to tap into those talents. The talents that come from the Father can be accessed by people who know and love him and those he has found to be trustworthy. I'm not going to tell you what his talents are, because that's for you to discover. You get to learn about him.

You can learn about his talents when the following happens:

- The Lord trusts you.

- You are faithful to him.

- You stay strong in him.

- You hold on to him through your trials, temptations, and testings.

You will find that the Lord will start to give you access to his talents, the talents that reside within him. You can't get any greater exploration or resource of talent than what Father God has. He has the highest giftings. If you want excellence in your craft, in your giftings, and in your talents, then go to the Father and access him. You can be operating with him on earth, accessing his talents and his abilities and doing great things that people who aren't connected to God can't do. It's in your best interests to know the love of the Father, to explore his talents, and to know his blessings. He always wants to bless you; he always wants to shower his love upon you. He has so much to give and offer you. He will never harm you.

I know, Nicola, that you have often thought about the statement in C. S. Lewis's series the Chronicles of Narnia: *The Lion, the Witch and the Wardrobe.*

Mr. Beaver says that Aslan, who represents the Father God and Jesus, is not safe, but he is good.[1] Well, I want to tell you that the Father is safe. Even when Jesus was on the cross, you could say that the Father was not safe; he let the Son go through so much suffering. But the Father was helping the Son when he was on the cross. The Father kept him safe and gave him the peace and the security he needed in the Father's love so that he could endure that horrible pain. God gave Jesus everything he needed to get through that terrible experience. God is safe because he provided the love; he provided the endurance to get Christ through the cross. He reminded Jesus and showed him the thousands and millions and billions of people who would come to him through what he was doing. In this way, Jesus could be encouraged on the cross. (See Hebrews 12:2.) The Father helped Jesus to get through what he went through. Jesus held his arms out to the world while the Father was holding Jesus in his arms.

Nicola: Thank you, Enoch. Would you like to say anything more to people who aren't Christians about what God is like?

---

[1] C.S. Lewis, *The Lion, the Witch and the Wardrobe* (Glasgow: William Collins & Co. Ltd., 1988), 75.

Enoch: He is a loving Father. He would never harm his children. He doesn't harm them. He allows evil in the world, but he is always working for their good. When Satan is afflicting someone, God is pouring mercy, love, endurance, strength, hope, and optimism on that person at the same time. God's love and endurance, peace, and faith always overwhelm and outdo the evil coming against that person. God is always good, Nicola. God is always good.

Nicola: Thank you, Enoch. Do you have any additional words for people who aren't Christians?

Enoch: I would say, Nicola, that God is loyal. He will never let you down. He is even loyal to those who aren't loyal to him. He is loyal to those who call themselves Christians but who then murder their spouses or children. He forgives them, washes them, sets them free, and gives them a new start. He doesn't turn his back on those who cry out to him. Just like King David, who slept with Bathsheba and then murdered her husband, Uriah; God received David back, just like that, when David cried out in repentance to him. The Lord is loyal, loyal to those who are his. Even murder isn't too much for God to restore, redeem, and forgive. God can undo the evil in what has been done. So, yes, I would say that God is loyal; he will never harm or hurt. Just as it is in his nature to do good, he will only ever do good to you. That's all I have to say on that question. Thank you, Nicola.

QUESTION 4:

What do you have to say to Christian men?

Enoch: Well, Nicola, first I want to say to you that Christian men have a really difficult life these days. The days are harsh and cruel and provide lots of temptations for men. I don't envy the men of this age. Although God is doing great things in this generation, I don't envy the struggles, the temptations, the stress, and the anxiety that come upon the sons of men. Men need to hear that they have someone on their side, someone who doesn't condemn them but who loves them and understands their struggles. Jesus and God are not up in heaven looking down and saying, "Oh, woe to you, you terrible man. You just looked at pornography. Oh, woe to you, you terrible man. You just hit your wife; you just yelled at your children; you cheated at work."

He's asking, "How can I help? How can I come into your life? How can I transform you? How can I show you that I love you? How can I be the God, the Father, to you that you need, the father that you didn't have? I want to be that father to you."

He's not looking down and condemning them or thinking that they're such a mess that he can't use them.

He's saying, "I want to transform that mess, and I don't see you as a mess. I see that you have been created for great and mighty things. The mess does not disqualify you. In fact, I can use the mess. When I have transformed you, you can help other people escape their messes too."

I want a company of restoring redeemers, a company of people who can do amazing things for the Lord. I will be working with the sons of men when I am one of the two witnesses on this earth. Just like God, I want to see men restored, redeemed, and delivered from their situations. It's no surprise that men are struggling these days, because the enemy has brought so much against them, because he sees the great callings upon their lives and the great exploits they will do. He sees the healing that they will bring into the lives of other men and into the next generation.

The enemy is trying whatever he can. He is placing stress on them, which is almost too hard to bear. He is trying to cut their destinies short and to stop them from dealing with their problems. He's trying to make them think that they can't take it anymore. He wants them to jump off bridges or stab themselves or overdose on medication. He wants to bring them to the point of such desperation that they think, "It's too much. I can't do this." So they go off into drinking or drugs or some sort of addiction. That's the enemy's plan.

But these overwhelming feelings that men have that they can't take anymore are almost the Lord's intentions so that they will turn to him. The Lord would say to men that he wants them to turn to him because when they're overwhelmed and when they can't take anymore, that's when God can use, transform, and heal them. This time of weakness becomes their greatest strength. God can absolutely restore them. The Lord can begin a healing work where he can do great exploits through them. Then the Lord can use them to heal other men and young boys who are struggling as well.

That's what I would say to men. I would say that their future is bright in the Lord. Yes, many men on this earth at the moment are struggling terribly, and not all of them know that there's an answer. I want all the Christians who read this book to get the message out to men: to non- Christian men in their workplaces and to their struggling friends who don't know Christ. Let them know that God has a great future for them and that if they just turn to God in their stress and in their feelings of desperation, he can do amazing things. He can restore them. They will turn out better than they could think. They will do things that they would never imagine they would do. They just have so much potential within them. Those who are struggling greatly and those who the enemy is coming against the hardest are the ones the Lord will use the most. That's all I have to say for that question, Nicola. Thank you.

QUESTION 5:

What do you have to say to Christian women?

Enoch: I would say, Nicola, that women can be very delicate. Their femininity is very well expressed in the world today. Women like to look beautiful and dress up with clothes, shoes, and bags. But my message to them is that it's not all about the outward appearance or about them looking attractive to men. Sure, they can look their best, but they must have the heart of the Proverbs 31 woman and be faithful to God and seek him. They shouldn't believe the media message that tells them to dress like people in the magazines or have a certain size waist or bust. They shouldn't have to go through plastic surgery because the Lord loves them as they are. The Lord wants them to know that he accepts them as they are.

He really wants them to accept themselves and dress nicely but not to worry too much about their appearance. The Lord created them, and he says that what he has created is good. The Lord would say to women that he has them covered; he has their backs; he is calling them beautiful, wonderful, and marvellous, and he really wants them to focus on God's will for their lives. He wants them to seek him first and not seek to please man, men, their men, or their husbands. They should seek to please their husbands and to get along with them but not to the extent that they become insecure in their relationships with them. They should not be so insecure that they constantly strive to please them or that they can't accept themselves. That's not healthy.

They need to accept themselves in the Lord and dress well but not worry too much about it. They should seek to help their husbands, focus on how they can serve the Lord, find their spiritual gifts, and work on developing them. They should find their talents in the Lord and put them to work, show others the way of faith and bring up the next generation, and encourage and mentor younger women and girls in what they have learned: that it's not all about appearance but about pleasing the Lord's heart and about having a pure, lovely, and gentle spirit. It's about having purity, a pureness of life, before him.

It's about being sold out, much as Heidi Baker is. She dresses well, but she doesn't stress about her appearance. She looks beautiful, but she doesn't make her appearance—high heels, fancy clothes, or the latest fad—the primary goal of her life. Unfortunately, so many women become caught up in this, and they never feel acceptable, no matter how hard they try. They don't like the look or the feel of some part of their body. And I would tell them that they just need to accept themselves. They need to exercise and do their best. The bodies that the Lord has given them are acceptable to him, and if other people don't like their bodies, they need to remember that the Lord has accepted them. They need to accept and love themselves as they are. They need to know that they are loved by the Lord.

So, yes, women, pursue the talents that the Lord has given you. Glorify the Lord with your talents. Teach and mentor the next generation. Show an interest in other young women, and point them in the right direction, just as I have pointed you in the right direction.

That's all I have to say on that today, Nicola. Thank you for that question.

QUESTION 6:

How would a person qualify to be taken from this earth without death, such as the hope of Christians going in the rapture?

Enoch: Be pure in heart, Nicola. Be pure in heart and follow the Lord to the best of your ability. Pour your life into the Lord and your heart and your life into others. Pour yourself into God, and just be completely sold out to him. As you read in Matthew's book *Princess Diana Speaks from Heaven*, Diana's completely in love with and sold out to the Lord.

You are worthy to be taken in the rapture if you meet the following qualifications:

- You have a bold faith.
- You have an intimate relationship.
- Your heart is completely in love with the Lord.
- Your heart is strong in the Lord.
- You have managed to keep true to your declaration of belief in the Lord without denying him.

Enduring what you have had to suffer without trying to escape your pain is part of embracing the cross of Christ. If you have gone through tribulation or difficulty in your personal life and have kept a pure heart while continuing to love others and doing the right thing, you are worthy to be taken in the rapture. If you have done what the Lord has asked you to do, have a pure conscience before him, and have confessed your sins, you are worthy to be taken from this earth without death.

As you know, I left the earth without experiencing death. That was not just because I lived a holy and worthy life but because God had a future plan for me as one of the two witnesses who will come back to earth. As long as you keep your heart pure before the Lord and do everything that he has told you to do, you are on track. If you refuse to do what he has told you to do, then you need to clear your conscience and do what the Lord says. If you're having trouble doing what he says, you need to get some support, help, or counseling so that you can obey him. Outside advice can help you be sure of what the Lord told you to do. You need to make sure that you're not being misdirected or that you haven't misunderstood and heard a different voice. If you are questioning what you heard, then maybe you need to check out if the Lord really said it. You need advisors for that. You need to talk with trusted people, and if they say, "Yes, I believe the Lord told you to do that," then you need to do it. But if they say, "No, I don't believe that was the voice of the Lord," then you can put that aside.

The Lord sometimes asks us to do hard things. If we can do those things, then we maintain a pure heart before him. Obedience is not taught much these days, but it is very important. When the Lord asks us to do something, he expects us to do it. For some of us, it will take a little bit longer to be obedient because we are human, and we are frightened. We are scared of people's perceptions, of their rejection, and of civil consequences. For example, if we are confessing a sin, such as adultery in a marriage, we might be afraid of the repercussions. Maybe we're afraid of losing a friendship or of being rejected. In all these things, God knows what he wants us to do, and he always has our best interests at heart.

If he's telling us to confess a sin or to share something with a person, then it will actually bring about good in our lives even if we are afraid. God has our best interests in mind, and we must trust God and do and say what he's asking us to do and say, even if it seems weird, odd, or strange. If we've checked it out with at least three other people and they say, "Yes, I think that's God," then do that thing, and just trust in the Lord for the outcome. Don't worry—if the worst happens, the worst happens, but the Lord has still asked you to do it, and he will turn everything around for good. Even if something negative happens, the Lord will make sure that something good comes from it: reconciliation or healing. You will have a clear conscience that you have done what the Lord has said to do.

You don't have anything to worry about if you have a pure heart, if you've been obedient to the Lord, if you've used your talents for him, if you're sold out for him, and if you love him. The Lord will honor you, and you will be blessed. You will be eligible to go in the rapture if you love your neighbor and you've forgiven him in Jesus's name. That's all I have to say on that, Nicola.

QUESTION 7:

Can you tell us what percentage of Christians are the Bride of Christ, and how do you become the Bride of Christ?

Enoch: Well, Nicola, I can't tell you the exact percentage that are the Bride of Christ, because the number is hidden from me. Only the Father knows. You become the Bride of Christ by making yourself ready and by preparing yourself for him.

Just as a bride prepares her garments, her heart, her vows, and everything for those who are coming to the ceremony, so the Lord wants you to be ready. He wants your heart to be ready; he wants your heart to be pure. He wants your emotional issues healed as much as possible. He wants you to come to him for healing and for blessing and to receive his love for you. He wants your love for him, and he wants your friendship. He wants you to forgive him for the times in your life where you've felt disappointed or hurt by him. Some people have an issue with that, saying that you don't have to forgive God because God can't do anything wrong. But the fact is that at times we become offended at God, and it becomes necessary for us to forgive God for our own emotional well-being.

We don't want anything in the way of a relationship between Jesus and his Bride. Yes, he wants our garments white, clean, and spotless. Every time we sin, he washes us and gives us clean garments. We must regularly confess sin. You don't have to be super worried or obsess about your sin. You don't have to focus or concentrate on it. It simply means that as soon as you are aware that you've fallen short of the Lord's standard, you've sinned. Confess it and then focus on doing better next time. You don't have to feel bad and think that you've let the Lord down or worry about what you did. If you focus on the sin, it will just make it worse. The Lord wants continual confession of sin. Take communion when you can, as often as possible. You will have a special time with him in heaven at the Marriage Supper of the Lamb if you are the Bride of Christ. You will dance with him, worship him, and eat at his table.

To be the Bride of Christ, you have to know Jesus and have a relationship with him. Jesus and God are currently giving you time to do this on earth—to learn how to hear their voices and have a relationship with them. It's not enough to know about God. You'll hear a lot of people say this, but you really have to get it in your heart. You actually need to be able to talk to Jesus and have him talk back to you. You can't have a relationship without communication and conversation. If you purchase Mark Holloway's book *The Freedom Diaries: God Speaks Back* or Matthew's book *How to Hear*

God's Voice: Keys to Conversational Two-Way Prayer, then you will learn more. Many books can teach you how to hear Jesus's voice. You just need to be determined. You can hear the voice of God and of Jesus.

Once you know Jesus and you are his Bride, then he will introduce you to the Father, and you can hear the Father's voice as well. It's very important to know and to love Jesus. Keep a short account of sins with him because you never know when you're going to die, when you'll be taken and your life will be over. You need to hear from him and know what he's asking you to do. You need to be obedient to him as I previously explained. You need to really know and love the Lord, and then you will be accepted as his Bride.

Nicola: Thank you, Enoch.

QUESTION 8:

Is there any need to fear the coming tribulation?

Enoch: Well, Nicola, that's a big subject, and I could say a lot about that. I know a lot about what is coming in the tribulation. A lot of theological questions and opinions are circulating out there as to what will happen: pretribulation, midtribulation, and posttribulation theories. I'm not going to go into which one of those is correct or what will happen. I will just say that if your heart is pure before the Lord, you don't need to fear the tribulation. Jesus will keep you safe. He has a plan for the saints, a plan to protect you until it's your time to go to heaven. You don't need to worry about going to heaven before your time. If you are in relationship with the Lord, hearing his voice, and following him, he will tell you exactly what to do to keep safe.

Christians will be living in communities, as Matthew has explained before in his book *Optimistic Visions of Revelation.*

They will be looking after each other and keeping each other close. They will be looking out for proverbial lost lambs, who need to be kept safe from the wolves. There's no need to fear the tribulation, because the Spirit of the Lord will be so strong. It's a bit like Kat Kerr's belief that Christians in this kingdom age will be ruling and reigning. Christians will be aspiring to do so many great things for the Lord: change the weather patterns and systems, impact the pervading evil in the outside world, and pull people back into the kingdom of God. They will be concentrating on so many things that they won't have time to fear the tribulation.

By the time the tribulation comes, the Lord will have removed the demonic stronghold of fear from the hearts and minds of Christians. It won't be a major problem. The enemy currently uses fear to disable and paralyze Christians. But when the tribulation comes, a great work will have been done by the Lord and by the Father, and fear will be squashed in Christians' lives. It won't be a major issue. Christians don't need to worry about fear, because the Lord has a plan to stop fear in its tracks. The enemy won't be able to use the weapon of fear, because the Lord will have practically wiped it out.

Since Christians will have no fear during this time, they will be great witnesses to the rest of the people of the world, who will be cowering and trembling in fear. When they see the faith, the hope, the strength, and the fearlessness of Christians, they will want to be like those Christians, and many, many people will come into the kingdom of God. The only people who will need to fear the tribulation are those who don't know the Lord. Those who are destined to come to know the Lord and to be part of the Bride of Christ will see these Christians: their devotion, how they look after each other, and how they love each other. They will come flooding into the Christian communities and churches, bringing a massive revival.

The people who weren't saved in the recent revival will come during the tribulation. Those people will be more difficult to win because they have harder hearts. They will tremble and fear because of what is coming on the earth. When they see such a clear difference between those who are not in the kingdom and those who are, they will want to become Christians and will soon become part of these communities. They will be some of the greatest evangelists for others outside the kingdom. So, Nicola, that is all I have to say on that question. Thank you for asking that. I hope that it is okay.

Nicola: Yes, Enoch, thank you very much.

QUESTION 9:

How did you reach the state of intimacy that you have attained?

Enoch: Well, it is quite simple to reach that level of intimacy. You have to want it. You have to be hungry. If you're not hungry, you need to be around Christian churches and people. You can catch hunger. You can see passion and zeal in others and want it for yourself. I would say that Christianity is more caught than it is taught. If you aren't hungry, you can ask the Lord for it. You can say, "Lord, I want to be hungry. I lack a desire to follow you or your ways, spend time with you, wait on you, and talk to you. Jesus, please change me." He will. He will be faithful to answer that prayer. He will make you hungry so that you desire him. He will change your circumstances so that you will turn to him and spend time with him.

And, oh, when you spend that time with Jesus, you will experience such sweet intimacy, and once you know him, you won't turn back or want to go back into the world. You'll have such a pure and beautiful relationship with the Father and with Jesus that you will not want to forget about him again. You will enjoy and look forward to spending time with Jesus and hearing what he has to say. It won't be a chore, but you will look forward to it. It won't be difficult for you, but it will be such a joy. Jesus and the Father really enjoy spending time with you. They can spend time with you in heaven. When I was on earth, I spent a lot of time in heaven with the Father. Heaven loved me, and they loved having me visit heaven until they finally kept me here one day.

As you begin to access the voice of the Father and Jesus, you'll begin to access heaven and see into realms of glory. And when you see the joy and the peace that is there, when you have that sweet relationship with Jesus, nothing will hold you back again. Nothing will make you want to turn back to the coldness, the harshness, and the emptiness of the physical world that you live in. You will want all of the Father, all of Jesus, and all of the Holy Spirit. You won't want anything more than the Father and Jesus. That's how you achieve the level of intimacy that I had with the Father. That's all I have to say about that. Thank you, Nicola.

QUESTION 10:

Are you unique in your relationship, or can anyone have a relationship with God like you?

Enoch: No, Nicola, I'm not unique. Anyone can have a relationship with God as I do, and many people on this earth today, including Matthew, do have that special relationship with God. Others have yet to be revealed to the world, but they have intimate knowledge of the Father and of Jesus. They will be used in mighty ways in this coming billion-soul harvest that Bob Jones prophesied about. There will be so much joy for those people with this type of relationship with God. It's certainly not out of reach for the average person or for the most or the least talented person. It's not out of reach for a millionaire or a billionaire or for the person who lives in a slum in India or Africa.

A relationship with God as I have is open and available to everyone. Nothing but your own desire and will can stop you from having this kind of relationship. In the last answer, I told you how to reach the state of intimacy that I had—through hunger and desire. You have to learn to take the time to discover the joy that you can have in a relationship with Jesus and the Father. You'll never go back once you've experienced it. It's very possible to have a relationship with God as I have. Don't let anything or anybody stop you.

The people in the persecuted countries, some of whom are sitting in jail, have a massive opportunity to really seek me out and to hear my voice, just like the Apostle John on the Island of Patmos. He was struggling in a labor camp. He had amazing revelations of heaven, which became the book of Revelation. People who are being tortured or who are in labor camps, even children, can use this time to develop intimacy with God. They can have a relationship with God as I did. All it takes is time. As I previously said, if you aren't hungry to spend time with God, but you want to be hungry for him, ask him for that hunger. God is faithful; he will always give you the hunger you need to seek him. You can have visions of heaven. You can go to heaven as I do.

Those people who are suffering the most on this earth can have a respite by visiting heaven. They can learn to see visions and to hear the voice of God. Nothing should stop a person. If you have such an intimate relationship with God that you visit heaven, one of the most important things you can do is to teach people how to know God as you do. Matthew does this. He has a tremendous relationship with the Father and with Jesus, and he communicates how he developed that relationship and what Jesus has said and done for him through the stories of his life. He is all about teaching other people how to know God intimately as he does. Even if you are not as close to God as Matthew or I are, you can teach a person who knows less than you. You can help the person next to you—a friend, a Christian, or a non-Christian—to have a hunger for the Lord. If you can motivate that person to seek the Lord, to have a conversation with him, then you will shine like the stars forever and ever. (See Daniel 12:3.) You will have led a person to the Lord, and you will cover many sins. And that's all I have to say on that one, Nicola.

41

Nicola: You have given me some amazing answers. I'm getting really tired, but I just pray the Lord will give me enough energy for this last question. I've had a wonderful interview with you, Enoch.

QUESTION 11:

Enoch, what are your final words?

Enoch: I would just say, Nicola, that I am so very proud of you for what you're doing with your prophecies. You're leading many people closer to the Lord. You've faced criticism and opposition from some of your friends, and I want you to know that the Lord sees this, and he will reward you for continuing to do what he has told you to do.

My final words to Christians all around the world would be to tell them to keep going, keep serving, keep pressing in, and keep persevering. They should never give up, because they only have one life, and they have only one chance to live this life on earth. They should make it their best life and be the best person they can be. The Lord loves those who seek after him. The Lord loves those who try to do his will and try to please him. It's not about being perfect but about doing the best they can, staying the course, running the race, and winning the prize. It's about doing the best job possible while here on earth.

It's not always easy, and I know that you'll sometimes feel like giving up, running away, or even taking your own life. I know you struggle at times, Nicola. But it's always worth persevering. I just want to say that something better is always coming around the corner. Things don't stay the same if you're going through hard times; they will change. What you're experiencing right now could end in two days, five weeks, or two months. Your circumstances could change at any time.

Make the most of what you have right now. If you have a working body, use that body, and if you have a working mind, use that mind. You don't know what will happen in the future. You don't know when the end of your life will come. Do your best all the time, keep short accounts before God, and love your brother and your sister. Love and honor your parents and be at peace with those around you. Be a peacemaker and spread the love of God wherever you can. You don't always have to share a sermon with people. You can just love and encourage them or be a friend to them. You don't have to be perfect.

You don't have to know all the answers to theological questions. Some apologists, such as Ravi Zacharias, seem to always have the right words to say. Sometimes you think, *Oh, I wish Ravi Zacharias were here; he could answer my friend's question perfectly*. You feel that you're not smart enough to answer that person's questions. Well, the thing is, you have a testimony, a life that's changed, which is enough to answer anyone's questions.

If you have a relationship with God, you can ask him what to say to people, and he can tell you what to say or how to serve, bless, or forgive them. He can tell you what he wants you to do for them. You can do so much on this earth to help bring others closer to Christ. Every seed you plant is watered by the Lord, and you will see in heaven just how much you have been rewarded by doing his will, by doing what he has asked you to do.

Some of you aren't close to the Lord, and you don't know how to communicate with him. You can learn this skill; it's not just for some people. You can learn how to hear the voice of God talking back to you. This gift is available to everyone, not just to the rich, the super spiritual, or pastors. Plenty of books or ministries out there will teach you how to hear the voice of God. Don't just rely on the minister at your church to tell you what God is saying. God wants to speak to you personally and give you answers for your everyday life. He wants to tell you what to say to that person at work or that family member. He wants to help you with that situation at home or with your drug-addicted son or daughter. He wants to tell you how much he loves you and take you into heaven. He wants so many things for you on this earth that all start with a relationship with him. I would encourage you to get to know him intimately.

And that's all I have to say to you, Nicola. It's been a pleasure speaking to you, and I hope you have a good night.

Nicola: Thank you so much, Enoch. I really loved this interview. It was so awesome. Thank you so much.

I'd Love to Hear from You!

One of the ways that you can bless me as a writer is by writing an honest and candid review of my book on Amazon. I always read the reviews of my books, and I would love to hear what you have to say about this one.

Before I buy a book, I read the reviews first. You can make an informed decision about a book when you have read enough honest reviews from readers. One way to help me sell this book and to give me positive feedback is by writing a review for me. It doesn't cost you a thing but helps me and the future readers of this book enormously.

To read my blog, request a life-coaching session, request your own personal prophecy, to receive a personal message from your angel, you can also visit my website at *http://personal-prophecy-today.com* All of the funds raised through my ministry website will go toward the books that I write and self-publish.

To write to me about this book or to share any other thoughts, please feel free to contact me at my personal email address at *survivors.sanctuary@gmail.com*

You can also friend request me on *Facebook at Matthew Robert Payne*. Please send me a message if we have no friends in common as a lot of scammers now send me friend requests.

You can also do me a huge favor and share this book on Facebook as a recommended book to read. This will help me and other readers.

How to Sponsor a Book Project

If you have been blessed by this book, you might consider sponsoring a book for me. It normally costs me between fifteen hundred and two thousand dollars or more to produce each book that I write, depending on its length.

If you seek the Holy Spirit about financing a book for me, I know that the Lord would be eternally grateful to you. Consider how much this book has blessed you and then think of hundreds or even thousands of people who would be blessed by a book of mine. As you are probably aware, the majority of my books are ninety-nine cents on Kindle, which proves to you that book writing is indeed a ministry for me and not a money-making venture. I would be very happy if you supported me in this.

If you have any questions for me or if you want to know what projects I am currently working on that your money might finance, you can write to me at *survivors.sanctuary@gmail.com* and ask me for more information. I would be pleased to give you additional details about my projects.

You can sow any amount to my ministry by simply sending me money via the PayPal link at this address: *http://personal-prophecy-today.com/support-my-ministry*.

You can be sure that your support, no matter the amount, will be used for the publishing of helpful Christian books for people to read.

Other Books by Matthew Robert Payne

What I Believe

Living for Eternity

Your Identity in Christ

7 Keys to Intimacy with Jesus

Finding Intimacy with Jesus Made Simple

Finding Your Purpose in Christ

Jesus Speaking Today

His Redeeming Love: A Memoir (Part 2)

The Parables of Jesus Made Simple: Updated and Expanded Edition

Christian Discipleship Made Simple

Nineteen Scriptures to Change Your Life Forever

Influencing your World for Christ: Practical Everyday Evangelism

Optimistic Visions of Revelation

How to Hear God's Voice: Keys to Conversational Two-Way Prayer

Conversations with God: Book 1

Conversations with God: Book 2

Conversations with God: Book 3

Getting Right with God: Exploring Intimacy through Daily Journaling and the Courts of Heaven

Twenty-Two Signs that You're Called to Be a Prophet

Deep Calls unto Deep: Answering Questions on the Prophetic

A Beginner's Guide to the Prophetic

The Prophetic Supernatural Experience

Prophetic Evangelism Made Simple

My Radical Encounters with Angels

My Radical Encounters with Angels: Book Two

A Message from My Angel: Book 1

Walking under an Open Heaven

My Visits to Heaven: Lessons Learned

Other Books by Matthew Robert Payne

Interviews with the Two Witnesses: Enoch and Elijah Speak

Apostle John Speaks from Heaven: A Divine Revelation

Apostle Paul Speaks from Heaven: A Divine Revelation

Apostle Peter Speaks from Heaven: A Divine Revelation

King David Speaks from Heaven: A Divine Revelation

Mary Magdalene Speaks from Heaven: A Divine Revelation

Mary Magdalene Speaks from Heaven Book 2: A Divine Revelation

Great Cloud of Witnesses Speak

Great Cloud of Witnesses Speak: Old and New

Great Cloud of Witnesses Speak: God's Generals

Great Cloud of Witnesses Speak: Interviews with Martha, Lazarus. Thomas and Timothy

My Visits to the Galactic Council of Heaven

Princess Diana Speaks from Heaven: A Divine Revelation

Michael Jackson Speaks from Heaven

Coping with your Pain and Suffering

Gaining Freedom from Sex Addictions: Breaking Free of Pornography and Prostitutes

Writing and Self-Publishing Christian Nonfiction

Five Keys to Successful Writing: How I Write One Book per Month

Visit Matthew Robert Payne's author page on Amazon at:

https://www.amazon.com/Matthew-Robert-Payne/e/B008N9R896

Upcoming Books

13 Tips to Becoming the Light of Christ

Simple Answers to Your Questions on the Prophetic

Acknowledgments

MATTHEW

Jesus:

I want to thank you for being my lifelong friend and for never deserting me, no matter how dark my life became. You led me into some great adventures, such as interviewing saints from heaven.

Holy Spirit:

I want to thank you for leading and teaching me. You are a great teacher, better than I could ever be. You have been with me every step of the way. Even as I do this book, you are with me to still my nerves.

Father:

Thank you for loving me and entrusting me with this life that I am living. Thank you for revealing my purpose to me and leading me toward accomplishing it. Thank you so much for your Son, Jesus. Thank you for everything that you have done in my life.

Lisa Thompson:

I want to give special thanks to Lisa for editing this book of mine. You take my simple words and transform them to make me seem smarter than I really am. If you have any editing needs, Lisa can be contacted at *writebylisa@gmail.com.*

Nicola:

I want to thank my co-author, Nicola, for having the courage to do this book with me. I want to thank you for being part of my team as a proofreader. I want to thank you for all the work that you did with this book to polish and improve it.

Friends:

I want to thank Darla, Lisa, Nicola, Mary, Wendy, Laura, David Joseph, and Michael Van Vlymen for your friendship and for how you have impacted my life.

Mom and Dad:

I want to thank my mother and father for all the love that they have given me. I am a product of your love.

Readers and Ministry Supporters:

I want to thank the readers of my books and my ministry supporters for the funds that you have given me to publish books. I want to thank the anonymous ministry supporter who gave me money for this project. I live to educate people, and I thank my readers and the supporters of my ministry because you make life worth living.

NICOLA

Father, Son, and Holy Spirit:

Thank you for guiding me through this process and offering never-ending love and support.

Mentors:

I'm thankful for some of the important people who have counseled me over the years, including Linda, Rae, Glenis, Raewyn, Ferrell, and Ros. Glenis and Rae, you have gone on to be with the Lord and received your reward. You have helped bring me to health and make me the person I am today.

Friends:

I'm thankful for my friends: Kathleen, Cheryl, Chrissy, Christina, Evelyn-Faith, Matthew, Dan, Levi, Jen, Caroline, Jan, Hailey, and many others.

Lisa Thompson & Megan Langston:

Special thanks to Lisa Thompson for editing this book and to Megan Langston for proofreading my section.

Family:

Thank you to my family for your unconditional love.

About the Authors

MATTHEW ROBERT PAYNE

Matthew Robert Payne, a teacher and prophet, enjoys writing what the Lord puts on his heart. He receives great pleasure from interacting with others on Facebook, hearing from people who have read his books, and prophesying over others. He is a passionate lover and disciple of Jesus Christ. He hopes that as you discover his books, you will intimately come to know Jesus, the Father, and Matthew himself though his transparent writing style.

Matthew grew up in a traditional Baptist church and gave his heart to Jesus Christ at the tender age of eight years old. But when he left home at the age of eighteen, he lived a wild life for many years. At twenty-seven, he was baptized in water and at the same time, baptized in the Holy Spirit. Matthew learned about the five-fold ministry offices and received a revelation of their value today.

He started his journey as a prophet twenty years ago, learning about this gift and putting it into practice. With thousands of prophecies under his belt, he can confidently prophesy to friends and strangers alike. He has been writing for a number of years and self-published his first book in 2011. Today he spends his time earning money to self-publish and writes a new book approximately every month.

Matthew writes simply from his life experience. He picks up information to share in his books from the reading that he does for his own personal growth. He relies on the Holy Spirit to give him verses to share as he writes instead of searching for scriptures to support his points. He is very real, authentic, and honest in his writing and in what he shares with readers.

You can connect with him on Facebook. You can sow into his book-writing ministry, read his blog, receive a message from your angel or even receive your own nine-minute personal prophecy from Matthew at *http://personal-prophecy-today.com.*

NICOLA WHITEHALL

A prophet and writer, Nicola has struggled for several decades with her overall health, so she understands people who have suffered. God brought her significant healing through focused therapy from 2007 to 2014. She plans to share more about her experiences in future writing. She also wants to address anxiety, healing from sexual and emotional abuse, and more as well as shine a light on how effective therapy can bring about growth and healing.

In 2018, she coauthored her first book with Matthew Robert Payne, *Mary Magdalene Speaks from Heaven, Book 2: A Divine Revelation.* She hopes that her books will stretch your mind, help you embrace new things, and touch your heart. You can request a prophecy from her for a donation at *http://personal-prophecy-today.com.* She enjoys dancing ballet and contemporary dance in her spare time.

www.ingramcontent.com/pod-product-compliance
Lightning Source LLC
Chambersburg PA
CBHW021943040426
42448CB00008B/1207